WISDOM

25 FACTS ABOUT WISDOM

ALPHONSO CRAWFORD

WISDOM

25 FACTS ABOUT WISDOM

ISBN 978-0-935379-13-6

Library of Congress Control Number: 2016903140

Published by New Life Educational Services
P.O. Box 96
Oak Lawn, Illinois 60454

Books are available from: Amazon.com

Printed in the U.S.A.

Contents

INTRODUCTION

If wisdom is to be described in a general perspective, Wisdom is the inner ability to know what to do, how to do and when to do a particular thing. Many people from different parts of the world can describe wisdom in various ways based on their level of revelation or manner of understanding. Wisdom from the spiritual angle can be defined as the supernatural ability to know what, how and when to do a particular thing or address a specific matter *Ex.36:1; Then wrought Bezaleel and Aholiab, and every wise hearted man, in whom the LORD put wisdom and understanding to know how to work all manner of work for the service of the sanctuary, according to all that the LORD had commanded.* Wisdom is basically of two types which are:

- Wisdom of man

- Wisdom of God.

Wisdom of man:

1cor. 2:1-6; [1] *And brethren, when I came to you, came not with excellency of speech or of wisdom, declaring unto you the testimony of God.* [2] *For I determined not to know anything among you, save Jesus Christ, and him crucified.* [3] *And I was with you in weakness, and in fear, and in much trembling* [4] *And my speech and my preaching [was] not with enticing words of man's wisdom, but in demonstration of the Spirit and of power:* [5] *that your faith should not stand in the wisdom of men, but in the power of God.* [6] *Howbeit we speak wisdom among them that are perfect: yet not the wisdom of this world, nor of the princes of this world, that come to nought:*

According to the scriptures, the wisdom of man is derived from the senses which have three different sources which are; man himself (sourced from the knowledge of the tree of good and evil), world (sourced from different media programs and social communications etc.), prince of this world (sourced from operational or governing spirits in the second heaven). Wisdom of man is based on what man can see, feel, hear, taste and smell. The wisdom of man has the following characteristics according to *James 3:13-16; [13] who [is] a wise man and endued with knowledge among you? Let him show out of a good conversation his works with meekness of wisdom. [14] But if ye have bitter envying and strife in your hearts, glory not, and lie not against the truth. [15] This wisdom descended not from above, but [is] earthly, sensual, and devilish. [16] For where envying and strife [is], there [is] confusion and every evil work.*

- Earthly

- Sensual

- And devilish.

Wisdom of God: there is a form of wisdom that comes from above, it is divine and powerful. The wisdom of God is based on revelation knowledge and found in the Spirit. *1cor.2:7-8; but we speak the wisdom of God in a mystery, [even] the hidden [wisdom], which God ordained before the world unto our glory: [8] which none of the princes of this world knew: for had they known [it], they would not have crucified the Lord of glory.* The wisdom of God is the very intent of God searched by the Holy Spirit and being revealed to us by the Spirit. This wisdom has the following characteristics; *James 3:17; But the wisdom that is from above is first pure, then peaceable, gentle, [and] easy to be entreated, full of mercy and good fruits, without partiality, and without hypocrisy.*

- Pure

- Peaceable

- Gentle

- Easily entreated

- Full of mercy and good fruits

- Is without partiality and hypocrisy.

In this study our focus would be on the wisdom that comes from above which is the wisdom of God.

FACTS ABOUT THE WISDOM OF GOD

1. WISDOM IS A PERSON

1cor. 1:24; ... but to those who are called, both Jews and Greeks, Christ the power of God and the wisdom of God.

Those who are called and sanctified, who received the gospel, and are enlightened by the Spirit of God, they develop, and discern more glorious discoveries of God's wisdom and power in the doctrine of Christ crucified than in all his other works. Note that, those who are saved are reconciled to the doctrine of the cross, and led into an acquaintance with the mysteries of Christ crucified. Christ is the wisdom of God to those that are called both Jews and gentiles; but to them that are not called, Christ crucified is a stumbling-block to the Jews. They could not get over it. They had a conceit that their expected Messiah was to be a great temporal prince, and therefore would never own one who made so lowly an appearance in life, and died so accursed a death, for their deliverer and king. They despised him, and looked upon him as deplorable because he was hanged on a tree, and because he did not gratify them with a sign though his divine power shone out in innumerable miracles. The Jews always require a sign to believe this wisdom. *(1Cor. 1:22. See Matt.12:38.)* And to the unbelieving gentiles, the crucifixion was foolishness. They laughed at the story of a crucified Savior, and despised the apostles' way of telling it. They sought for wisdom. They were men of wit and reading, men that had cultivated the arts and sciences, and had, for several ages, been in a manner the very mint of knowledge and learning. There was nothing in the plain doctrine of the cross to suit their taste, nor humor their vanity, nor gratify a curious and wrangling temper: they entertained it therefore with scorn and contempt. What, hope to be saved by one that could not save himself! And trust in one who was condemned and crucified as a malefactor, a man of low birth and poor condition in life, and cut off by so vile and opprobrious a death! This was what the pride of human reason and learning could not relish. The Greeks thought it little better than stupidity to receive such a doctrine, and pay this high regard to such a person: and thus were they justly left to perish in their pride and obstinacy. Note, it is just with God to leave those to themselves who pour such proud contempt on divine wisdom and grace. The wisdom that comes from above is a person that is Christ. *1Cor. 1:30, But of Him you are in Christ Jesus, who became for us wisdom from God-and righteousness and sancti ication and redemption.*

Of him and out of his free will by grace and mercy we were engrafted into Christ Jesus, who is made unto us wisdom, who were before utterly foolish and ignorant of the God head and his spiritual operation. His person as the wisdom of God is all we need, or could ever desire. Man is foolish, ignorant and blind in the things of God, with all our boasted knowledge; and he is made wisdom to us. We are guilty, obnoxious to justice; and he is made righteousness, our great atonement and sacrifice. We are depraved and corrupt; and he is made sanctification, the spring of our spiritual life; from him, the head, it is communicated to all the members of his mystical body by his Holy Spirit. We are in bonds, and he is made redemption to us, our Savior and deliverer. Observe, Where Christ is made righteousness to any soul, he is also made sanctification. He never discharges from the guilt of sin, without delivering from the power of it; and he is made righteousness and sanctification, that he may in the end be made complete redemption, may free the soul from the very being of sin, and loose the body from the bonds of the grave: and what is designed in all is that all flesh may glory in the Lord As Christ-like, we have the same inheritance of God because we are joint-heirs with Christ *(Romans 8:17)*. So we have the fullness of wisdom, who is Jesus Christ. Consider how great was the "wisdom of Solomon" that it was inspired by God and placed in the Holy Scriptures. How good it would be for the man who adheres to that advice. How noble and renowned that "The queen of the south shall rise up in judgment with the men of this generation, and condemn them: for she came from the utmost parts of the earth to hear the Wisdom of Solomon; and behold, a greater than Solomon is here" *Luke 11:31; A greater than Solomon's wisdom is here*. That is the person of Christ, the wisdom of God in whom the fullness of God dwells bodily. *(Col. 2:9)*.

2. WISDOM IS MEEK

James 3:13: who is a wise man and endued with knowledge among you? Let him show out of a good conversation his works with meekness of wisdom.

The scripture makes us understand that Christ as being made unto us wisdom *(1 Cor. 1:30)*. Remember it did not say Christ has given us wisdom, Christ is the wisdom and power of God *(1 Cor.1:24; but to those who are called, both Jews and Greeks, Christ the power of God and the wisdom of God)*...you must also understand that Christ as the wisdom of God was referred to as a meek man during his work on earth *(Matt.11:29, Matt.21:5 2Cor 10:1)*,therefore we cannot separate meekness from wisdom in fact, the meek is the wise and the wise is the meek.

What is meekness? There has been different meanings and definitions of the word meekness according to the context in which it is used, let me give you a simple, precise and a scriptural definition of meekness. Meekness is the state, position, attitude, expression and overflow of the heart which makes it lowly, or simply a state of being lowly in heart. Every other meaning can be coined out of this definition. Jesus Christ said in *(Matt 11:29)* that he is meek and lowly in heart...so, if Christ equals wisdom and meekness equals Christ then you agree with me that wisdom equals meekness. Christ neglecting his glory in heaven and coming in the likeness of man is a good example of being meek *(Phil.2:5-6; Let this mind be in you which was also in Christ Jesus, [6] who, being in the form of God, did not consider it robbery to be equal with God)*. This is to say that meekness cannot be separated from wisdom, in fact to be full of wisdom is to be meek.

The more wisdom you have, the more you develop a meek spirit, remember that meekness is a fruit of the spirit *(Gal 5:23)* but this is not a manifestation in the soul, but you need to receive the wisdom of God which is in the word to cause a work on your soul that the soul might be able to bear this same fruit. Therefore the more you receive of the wisdom of God, the more you become meek or humble.

3. WISDOM IS THE PRINCIPAL THING

Prov. 4:7; Wisdom is the principal thing; therefore get wisdom. And with all thy getting, get understanding.

By principal thing, the bible describes wisdom as the most important, head of all, the beginning of all. Wisdom is the beginning process and the end of all things. Therefore anything done outside of wisdom is not of God. Wisdom is the master of every situation.

4. WISDOM HAS TWO HANDS

Prov. 3:16; Length of days is in her right hand, in her left hand riches and honor.

Wisdom is here represented as a bright and bountiful queen, reaching forth with gifts to her faithful and loving subjects, and offering them to all that will submit to her government and lordship. Is length of days a blessing? Yes, the most valuable; life includes all good, and therefore she offers that in her right hand. Christianity puts us into the best way and manner of prolonging life, entitles us to the promises of it, and, though our days on earth should be no more than our neighbor's, yet it will secure to us everlasting life in the age to come. Are riches and honor accounted blessings? They are so, and these she reaches out with her left hand. For, she is ready to embrace those that submit to her with both arms, so she is ready to give out to them with both hands. They shall have the wealth of this world as far as Infinite Wisdom sees well for them *(Gen.18:18)*; while the true riches, by which men are rich towards God, are secured to them. Nor is there any honor, by birth or preferment, comparable to that which proceeds from Christianity; it makes the righteous more excellent than his neighbor, recommends men to God, commands respect and veneration with all the sober part of mankind, and will in the age to come make those that are now buried in obscurity to shine forth as the sun. Is pleasure courted as much as anything? It is so, and it is certain that true piety has in it the greatest true pleasure. Her ways are ways of pleasantness; the ways in which she has directed us to walk are such as we shall find abundance of delight and satisfaction in. All the enjoyments and entertainments of sense or that which enjoyment to our senses by stimulated happiness are not comparable to the pleasure which gracious souls have in communion with God and doing good. That which is the only right way to bring us to our journey's end we must walk in, fair or foul, pleasant or unpleasant; but the way of Christianity, as it is the right way, so it is a pleasant way; it is smooth and clean, and strewed with roses: All her paths are peace. There is not only peace in the end, but peace in the way; not only in the way of Christianity in general, but in the particular paths of that way, in all her paths, all the several acts, instances, and duties of it. One does not embitter what the other sweetens, as they relieve the world; but they are all peace, not only sweet, but safe. Wisdom is her name, identity and nature.

5. WISDOM IS GIVEN TO THOSE THAT ASK FOR IT

Jame1:5; if any of you lack wisdom, let him ask of God, that giveth to all men liberally, and upbraideth not; and it shall be given him.

Prov.2:3; Yes, if you cry out for discernment, and lift up your voice for understanding, it is clear that wisdom is readily available to all and at the same time not readily available because it's for those who are in Christ and in him alone that wisdom can be found because he is the person of wisdom. Here is something in answer to every discouraging turn of the mind, when we go to God, under a sense of our own weakness and folly, to ask for wisdom. He to whom we are sent, we are sure, has it to give: and He is of a giving disposition, inclined to bestow this upon those who ask (Matt.7:7; Ask, and it will be given to you; seek, and you will find; knock, and it will be opened to you. Nor is there any fear of his favors being limited to some in this case, so as to exclude others, or any humble petitioning soul; for he gives to all men. If you should say you want a great deal of wisdom, a small portion will not help you, the apostle affirms, he gives liberally; and lest you should be afraid of going to him unreasonably, or being put to shame for your folly, it is added, he upbraided not. Ask when you will, and as often as you will, you will meet with no upbraiding. And if, after all, any should say, "This may be the case with some, but I fear I shall not succeed so well in my seeking for wisdom as some others may," let such consider how particular and express the promise: It shall be given him. Justly then must fools perish in their foolishness, if wisdom may be had for asking, and they will not pray to God for it. But, there is one thing necessary to be observed in our asking, namely, that we do it with a believing, steady mind: Let him ask in faith, nothing wavering. Therefore, God gives wisdom to those who ask in faith.

6. WISDOM BEGINS WITH FEAR

Prov. 1:1-7; [1] *The proverbs of Solomon son of David, king of Israel:* [2] *for gaining wisdom and instruction; for understanding words of insight;* [3] *for receiving instruction in prudent behavior, doing what is right and just and fair;* [4] *for giving prudence to those who are simple, knowledge and discretion to the young* [5] *let the wise listen and add to their learning, and let the discerning get guidance* [6] *for understanding proverbs and parables, the sayings and riddles of the wise.* [7] *The fear of the LORD is the beginning of knowledge, but fools despise wisdom and instruction.*

Proverbs 9:10 (NIV) The fear of the LORD is the beginning of wisdom, and knowledge of the Holy One is understanding.

Psalm 111:10 (NIV) The fear of the LORD is the beginning of wisdom; all who follow his precepts have good understanding.

Proverbs 14:27 (NIV) the fear of the LORD is a fountain of life, turning a person from the snares of death.

Proverbs 15:33 (NIV) Wisdom's instruction is to fear the LORD, and humility comes before honor. Fear is defined as a human emotion caused by an expectation of evil or impending danger. This fear is realized at a very early age. A child for example, fears falling and learns ways to protect himself or herself from danger. Fright, also connected with fear, is defined, sudden and violent fear; terror. These emotions however are not the fear that the Bible speaks of. Biblical fear, or the fear of God, and the fear that is in human emotions are in direct contrast.

The Fear of God is Not Fright; according to Luther "Being afraid of God is different from fearing God. The fear of God is a fruit of love, but being afraid of Him is the seed of hatred. Therefore we should not be afraid of God but should fear Him so that we do not hate Him whom we should love. . . . Therefore the fear of God is more aptly called reverence. For example, we revere those whom we love, honor, esteem, and fear to offend." Also Luther, writing on the fourth Commandment on *Ex. 20* "But honor is higher than mere love and includes a certain fear, which unites with love, and causes a man to fear offending them more than he fears the punishment. Just as there is fear in the honor we pay a sanctuary, and yet we do not flee from it as from a punishment, but draw near to it all the more. Such a fear mingled with love is the true honor; the other fear without any love is that which we have toward things which we despise or flee from, as we fear the hangman or punishment. There is no honor in that, for it is a fear without all love, nay, fear that has with it hatred and enmity. Of this we have a proverb of Jerome: What we fear, that we also hate. With such a fear God does not wish to be feared or honored, but with the first, which is mingled with love and confidence.

The fear of the Lord, whose name is revered, is not a fear of his judgments here or hereafter, but of his goodness and grace; it is a reverential affection for him (God), a fiducially fear of him, a fear of offending so good a Being as he is; and it includes all spiritual worship of him, inward and outward, private and public; and at this true wisdom begins; a man begins to be wise when he fears the Lord, and not till then; this is his highest wisdom, and this is, as it may be rendered, "the chief of all wisdom" Our reverence of him is so: The fear of the Lord is the beginning of wisdom. It is not only reasonable that we should fear God, because His name is reverend and his nature is holy, but it is advantageous to us. It is wisdom; it will direct us to speak and act as becomes us, in a consistency with ourselves, and for our own benefit. It is the head of wisdom that is (as we read it), it is the beginning of wisdom. Men can never begin to be wise till they begin to fear God; all true wisdom takes its rise from true spirituality, and has its foundation in it. Or, as some understand it, it is the master wisdom, and the most excellent, the first in dignity. It is the principal wisdom, and the principal of wisdom, to worship God and give honor to him as our Father and Master. Those manage well who always act under the government of his holy fear. Our obedience to him is so: A good understanding have all those that do his commandments. Where the fear of the Lord rules in the heart there will be a constant conscientious care to keep his commandments, not to talk of them, but to do them; and such have a good understanding. The reverence of God is the foundation of wisdom.

7. WISDOM IS BUILT ON SEVEN PILLARS

Prov. 9:1-10; Wisdom has built her house, she has hewn out her seven pillars;

Wisdom who is a person designed and built her house on seven hewn pillars done by its creative power. The seven pillars upon which the building of wisdom is built is written in the previous chapter of the book of proverb.

PILLAR 1: PRUDENCE

(Prov.8:12): I Wisdom dwell with prudence, not with carnal policy (the wisdom that is from above is contrary to that, (2Cor.1:12), but with true discretion, which serves for the right ordering of the conversation, that wisdom of the prudent which is to understand his way and is in all cases profitable to direct, the wisdom of the serpent, not only to guard from harm, but to guide in eating food. Wisdom dwells with prudence *(Hos. 14:9;* who is wise? Let him understand these things. Who is prudent? Let him know them. For the ways of the Lord are right; The righteous walk in them, But transgressors stumble in them) for prudence is the product of God and an ornament for the wise; and there are more witty inventions found out with the help of the scripture, both for the right understanding of God's providence and for the effectual countering of Satan's devices and the doing of good in our generation, than were ever discovered by the learning of the philosophers or the politics of statesmen. We may apply it to Christ himself; He dwells with prudence, for his whole undertaking is the wisdom of God in a mystery, and in it God abounds towards us in all wisdom and prudence. Christ found out the knowledge of that great invention, and a costly one it was to

him, man's salvation, by his satisfaction, an admirable expedient. We had found out many inventions for our ruin; he found out one for our recovery. The covenant of grace is so well ordered in all things that we must conclude that he who ordered it dwelt with prudence. *Prov.22:3; A prudent man foresees evil and hides himself, But the simple pass on and are punished.*

PILLAR 2: DISCRETION

Discretion is the power or ability to form and make plans. *Prov. 18:15; the heart of the prudent acquires knowledge, and the ear of the wise seeks knowledge.* With true discretion, which serves for the right ordering of the conversation, the wisdom of the prudent which is to understand his way and is in all cases profitable to direct, the wisdom of the serpent, not only to guard from harm, but to guide in eating food.

PILLAR 3: THE FEAR OF GOD

As said earlier about fear, *Proverbs 15:33 (NIV) Wisdom's instruction is to fear the LORD, and humility comes before honor.*

Fear is defined as a human emotion caused by an expectation of evil or impending danger. This fear is realized at a very early age. A child for example, fears falling and learns ways to protect himself or herself from danger. Fright, also connected with fear, is defined, sudden and violent fear; terror. These emotions however are not the fear that the Bible speaks of. Biblical fear, or the fear of God, and the fear that is in human emotions are in direct contrast. *(Is.33:6; Wisdom and knowledge will be the stability of your times, and the strength of salvation; the fear of the Lord is His treasure).* Fear (reverence) can be learned *Deut.4:10; especially concerning the day you stood before the Lord your God in Horeb, when the Lord said to me, 'Gather the people to Me, and I will let them hear My words, that they may learn to fear Me all the days they live on the earth, and that they may teach their children.'* True Christianity, consisting in the fear of the Lord, which is the wisdom before recommended, teaches men,

To hate all sin, as displeasing to God and destructive to the soul: The fear of the Lord is to hate evil, the evil way, to hate sin as sin, and therefore to hate every false way. Wherever there is an awe of God there is a dread of sin, as an evil, as only evil.

Particularly to hate pride and passion, those two common and dangerous sins. Conceit, pride and arrogance, are sins which Christ hates, and so do all those who have the Spirit of Christ; everyone hates them in others, but we must hate them in ourselves. The contrary mouth, peevishness towards others, God hates, because it is such an enemy to the peace of mankind, and therefore we should hate it.

PILLAR 4: COUNSEL

Prov.8:13; Counsel is mine, and sound wisdom; I am understanding, I have strength.

Prov. 19:20; Listen to counsel and receive instruction, that you may be wise in your latter days.

The fourth of the seventh pillars of wisdom is counsel. In the multitude of counsel there is safety. Counsel as described in the scripture above deals with wisdom in the latter days. Note that;

1. It is well with those that are wise in their latter end, wise for their

latter end, for their future state, wise for the age to come just like the five wise virgins, that are found wise when their latter end comes, wise virgins, wise builders, wise stewards, that are wise at length, and understand the things that belong to their peace, before they be hidden from their eyes. A carnal or worldly man at his end shall be a fool *(Jer. 17:11)*, but godliness will prove wisdom at last.

2. Those that would be wise in their latter end must hear counsel and receive instruction, in their beginnings and must be willing to be taught and be ruled (coming under the lordship of Christ), willing to be advised and reproved, when they are young. Those that would be stored in winter must gather in summer. To make a wise latter day, one must invest in the present wisdom of receiving counsel because purpose is established by counsel.

PILLAR 5: SOUND WISDOM

Prov. 8:14; Counsel is mine, and sound wisdom; I am understanding, I have strength.

Sound wisdom written in this particular verse of the scripture talks about working ability or substance. Most of the time, expectation and demands in the place of work makes one yearn for wisdom. Wisdom is built upon ability to substantiate. God himself lays

up for the righteous sound wisdom. *Prov. 2:7; He stores up sound wisdom for the upright; He is a shield to those who walk uprightly.* Sound wisdom is the fifth of seven pillars of wisdom.

PILLAR 6: UNDERSTANDING

Prov. 8:14; Counsel is mine, and sound wisdom; I am understanding, I have strength.

Wisdom speaks here and called herself understanding. The coming of wisdom to every believer is to bring knowledge and understanding; to make it clear and practicable. *Prov24:3, through wisdom a house is built, and by understanding it is established; the lord gives wisdom and out of his mouth proceeds knowledge and understanding.* For every man that gets wisdom finds understanding. The relationship and connection between wisdom and understanding is clearly explained in *Prov. 7:4; Say to wisdom, "You are my sister," And call understanding your nearest kin.* To whom thou art nearly allied, and for whom thou hast a pure affection; call her thy friend, whom thou company." We must make the word of God familiar to us, consult it, and consult its honor, and take a pleasure in conversing with it.

PILLAR 7: POWER

Prov. 8:14; Counsel is mine, and sound wisdom; I am understanding, I have strength.

Eccl. 7:19; Wisdom strengthens the wise More than ten rulers of the city.

Wisdom teaches us not to expect that those we deal with should be faultless; because we ourselves are not so, none are so, no, not the best. This wisdom strengthens the wise as much as anything you could think about, and arms them against the danger that arises from provocation, so that they are not put into any form of disorder by it. They consider that those they have dealings and conversation with are not incarnate angels (being expected to be excellent in all things), but sinful sons and daughters of Adam: even the best are so, insomuch that there is not a just man upon earth, that does good and sins not, *Eccl. 7:20.* Solomon had this in his prayer *(1Ki. 8:46),* in his proverbs *(Pro. 20:9),* and here in his preaching. It is the character of just men that they do well; for the tree is known by its fruits. *Jer. 51:15; He*   24 *has made the earth by His power; He has established the world by His wisdom, and stretched out the heaven by His understanding. Explains the strong connection between wisdom and power.* The nature of wisdom is power. Power is the seventh pillar of wisdom.

8. WISDOM IS ONE OF THE SEVEN SPIRITS OF GOD

Is.11:1-2; There shall come forth a Rod from the stem of Jesse, And a Branch shall grow out of his roots.[2] The Spirit of the Lord shall rest upon Him, The Spirit of wisdom and understanding, The Spirit of counsel and might, The Spirit of knowledge and of the fear of the Lord. Wisdom is a spirit (among the seven spirits of God); because God is spirit and the things of God are spiritual as well. Paul prayed for the Ephesians Church that God should give them the spirit of wisdom and revelation in the knowledge of Him that their eyes of understanding may be enlightened *(Eph. 1:17-18;[17] that the God of our Lord Jesus Christ, the Father of glory, may give to you the spirit of wisdom and revelation in the knowledge of Him, [18] the eyes of your understanding being enlightened; that you may know what is the hope of His calling, what are the riches of the glory of His inheritance in the saints,).*

The spirit of wisdom thus does this:

The spirit gives illumination (Photizo), light in our life *(Eph. 1:18)*

The spirit of wisdom gives counsel/direction/guidance/advice *(Acts 16:6)*

The spirit of wisdom gives insight into secrets and mystery.

9. WISDOM BUILDS

Prov.24:3; through wisdom a house is built, and by understanding it is established;

We are tempted to envy those that grow rich, and raise their estates and families, by such unjust courses as our consciences will by no means suffer us to use. But, to set aside that temptation, Solomon here shows that a man, with prudent management, may raise his estate and family by lawful and honest means, with a good conscience, and a good name, with the blessings of God upon his industry; and, if the other be raised a little sooner, yet these will last a great deal longer. That which is here recommended to us as having the best influence upon our outward prosperity is wisdom, and understanding, and knowledge; that is, both piety towards God (for that is true wisdom) and prudence in the management of our outward affairs. We must govern ourselves in everything by the rules of Christianity first and then of discretion. Some that are truly pious do not thrive in the world, for want of prudence; and some that are prudent enough, yet do not prosper, because they lean to their own understanding and do not acknowledge God in their ways; therefore both must go together to complete a wise man. That which is here set before us as the advantage of true wisdom is that it will make men's outward affairs prosperous and successful. It will build a house and establish it. Men may by unrighteous practices build their houses, but they cannot establish them, for the foundation is rotten *(Hab. 2:9, Hab. 2:10)*; whereas what is honestly got will wear like steel and be an inheritance to children's children. It will enrich a house and furnish it. House here may never be a physical building alone but much more.

10. WISDOM IS A SPIRIT IN MAN

Job 32:1-9; [1] so these three men ceased answering Job, because he was righteous in his own eyes. [2] Then the wrath of Elihu, the son of Barachel the Buzite, of the family of Ram, was aroused against Job; his wrath was aroused because he justified himself rather than God.

[3] Also against his three friends his wrath was aroused, because they had found no answer, and yet had condemned Job. [4] Now because they were years older than he, Elihu had waited to speak to Job.

[5] When Elihu saw that there was no answer in the mouth of these three men, his wrath was aroused. [6] So Elihu, the son of Barachel the Buzite, answered and said: "I am young in years, and you are very old; therefore I was afraid, and dared not declare my opinion to you. [7] I said, 'Age should speak, and multitude of years should teach wisdom.' [8] But there is a spirit in man, and the breath of the Almighty gives him understanding. [9] Great men are not always wise, nor do the aged always understand justice.

According to this chapter of the scripture, many times we expect the aged to be wise in all things but it is not always so. Wisdom is a person and a spirit in man that the inspiration of God breathes upon to give the man understanding. But there is a spirit in man; only he expresses it a little more modestly, that one man has understanding as well as another, and no man can pretend to have the monopoly of reason or to engross all the trade of it. Had he meant I have revelation as well as you (as some understand it), he must have proved it; but, if he meant only I have reason as well as you, they cannot deny it, for it is every man's honor, and it is no presumption to claim it, nor could they gainsay his inference from it. Therefore hearken to me. Learn here, that the soul is a spirit, neither material itself nor dependent upon matter, but capable of conversing with things spiritual, which are not the objects of sense. It is an understanding spirit. It is able to discover and receive truth, to discourse and reason upon it, and to direct and rule accordingly. This understanding spirit is in every man; it is the light that lighteth every man, *John 1:9; that was the true Light which gives light to every man coming into the world.* It is the inspiration of the Almighty that gives us this understanding spirit; for he is the Father of spirits and fountain of understanding. For a better understanding, see *Gen. 2:7; Eccl. 12:7; Zech. 12:1.*That those who are advanced above others in grandeur and gravity do not always proportionally go beyond them in knowledge and wisdom because the spirit in every believer is a person of wisdom.

11. WISDOM DWELLS WITH THE ANCIENT

Job 12: 12-13; [12] *Wisdom is with aged men, And with length of days, understanding.* [13] *With Him are wisdom and strength, He has counsel and understanding.*

This is a noble discourse of Job concerning the wisdom, power, and sovereignty of God, in ordering and disposing of all the affairs of the children of men, according to the counsel of His own will, which none dare gainsay or can resist. Take both him and them out of the controversy in which they were so warmly engaged, and they all spoke admirably well; but, in that, we sometimes scarcely know what to make of them. It were well if wise and good men, that differ in their apprehensions about minor things, would see it to be for their honor and comfort, and the edification of others, to dwell most upon those great things in which they are agreed. On this subject Job speaks like himself. Here are no passionate complaints, no peevish reflections, but everything masculine and great.

He asserts the unsearchable wisdom and irresistible power of God. It is allowed that among men there is wisdom and understanding, *Job 12:12.* But it is to be found only with few, with the ancient, and those who are blessed with length of days, who get it by long experience and constant experience; and, when they have got the wisdom, they have lost their strength and are unable to execute the results of their wisdom. But now with God there are both wisdom and strength, wisdom to design the best and strength to accomplish what is designed. He does not get counsel or understanding, as we do, by observation, but he has it essentially and eternally in himself, *Job 12:13.* What is the wisdom of ancient men compared with the wisdom of the ancient of days! It is but little that we know, and less that we can do; but God can do everything, and no thought can be withheld from him. Happy are those who have this God for their God, for they have infinite wisdom and strength engaged for them. Foolish and fruitless are all the attempts of men against Him. Wisdom has been in existence before the beginning. It dwells with the ancient.

12. WISDOM IS SPOKEN IN THE MOUTH OF THE RIGHTEOUS

Ps. 37:30; the mouth of the righteous speaks wisdom, and his tongue talks of justice.

We must abound in good discourse, and with our tongues must glorify God and edify others. It is part of the character of a righteous man that his mouth speak wisdom; not only that he speaks wisely, but that he speaks wisdom, like Solomon himself, for the instruction of those around him. His tongue talks not of things idle and impertinent, but of judgment, that is, of the word and providence of God and the rules of wisdom for the right ordering of the conversation. Out of the abundance of a good heart will the mouth speak that which is good and to the use of edifying. We must have our wills brought into subjection to the will and word of God *(Psa. 37:31)*: The law of his God, is in his heart; and in vain do we pretend that God is our God if we do not receive his law into our hearts and resign ourselves to the government of it. It is but a jest and a mockery to speak of wisdom, and of judgment unless we have the law in our hearts, and we think as we speak. The law of God must be a commanding ruling principle in the heart; it must be a light there, a spring there, and then the conversation will be regular and appropriate: None of his steps will slide; it will effectually prevent backsliding into sin, and the uneasiness that follows from it. What is assured to us, as instances of our happiness and comfort, upon these conditions? That we shall have the blessing of God (wisdom), and that blessing shall be the spring, and sweetness, and security of all our temporal comforts and enjoyments. Such as are blessed of God, as all the righteous are, with a Father's blessing shall inherit the earth, or the land (for so the same word is translated, *Psa. 37:29*), the land of Canaan, that glory of all lands. The righteous speaks wisdom because they have the nature of wisdom which is righteousness. The person of wisdom dwells in the believers.

13. WISDOM MADE THE EARTH

Prov.3:19; The Lord by wisdom founded the earth; by understanding He established the heavens;

Jer. 10:12; He has made the earth by His power, He has established the world by His wisdom, and has stretched out the heavens by His discretion.

This description of wisdom should make us in love with the wisdom and understanding which God gives, that the Lord by wisdom founded the earth, so that it cannot be removed, nor can ever fail of answering all the ends of its creation, to which it is admirably and unexceptionably fitted. By understanding he has likewise established the heavens and directed all the motions of them in the best manner. The heavenly bodies are vast, yet there is no flaw in them - numerous, yet no disorder in them - the motion rapid, yet no wear or tear; the depths of the sea are broken up, and thence come the waters beneath the firmament, and the clouds drop down the dews, the waters from above the firmament, and all this by the divine wisdom and knowledge; therefore happy is the man that finds wisdom, for he will thereby be thoroughly furnished for every good word and work. Christ is that Wisdom, by whom the worlds were made and still consist; happy therefore are those to whom he is made of God wisdom, for he has wherewithal to make good all the foregoing promises of long life, riches, and honor; for all the wealth of heaven, earth, and seas, is his.

14. WISDOM HAS KINDS

Wisdom is one and he is a person but the dimension of operation is dynamic and it is stratified, that is it's in levels. The different kinds of wisdom will be discussed based on the original Greek word.

SOPHIA *(1Cor 2:6-12, Eph. 1:17-18)*

Sophia could be a worldly Sophia i.e. wisdom in devil's reality or a Godly Sophia i.e. wisdom in God's reality. And we will look into the Sophia of God because this is true wisdom. This kind of wisdom means insight into God's reality; seeing into God's truth; seeing with the perspective of God; having a knowing in the spiritual. Sophia is seeing and understanding in the line of God and with the mind of God. It is called the wisdom of God seen and understood of God's people. It is the wisdom that comes from knowing and understanding that 'This is what God said, This is what God does, This is how God works and This is the life of God. It is man's mind and thought in the knowledge of God. We can only have Sophia if we lock into the spiritual, catching or grasping the knowledge and holding unto what has been revealed to us by the spirit, even the deep things of God which a natural man cannot understand *(1Cor 2:11)*. As believers, we have this insight into these things because we are spiritual beings that discern the spiritual things of God.

SUNESIS *(Eph. 3:1-4,Col 1:9,2:2)*

Knowledge or understanding in these verses means Sunesis. Sunesis literally means mentally putting together, a uniting, a union, a bringing together; and it would be true to say that sunesis is that faculty of putting two and two together. Sunesis is called the CRITICAL WISDOM; the complete comprehension and perception which comes from understanding and analyzing the concepts and ideas and seeing the relationship between them. It is the power of distinguishing between different courses of action, different values of things, different relationships between people. Sunesis is the ability to test and to distinguish and to criticize and to evaluate and to form judgments. Sunesis is being able to put together those things that are spiritually discerned from SOPHIA and understand the relationship and correlation between them. It is the quickness in apprehension, and consideration which precedes action. A good application of Sunesis in the bible was when Daniel told king Nebuchadnezzar his dream, which the lord revealed to him in a night vision. Daniel got the insight into God's mind and he could comprehend and analyze this dream... Sunesis!!!(Dan 2:1-47) Therefore, we can say that sunesis is an interpreted Sophia.

PHRONESIS (Luke 1:17)

This is the wisdom that comes after the understanding and comprehension (sunesis) of the spiritual insight (Sophia); that is now made into actions or doings. This, in turn, becomes a way of life, pattern of living and procedure or method of doing and operating things which can be termed the MINDSET or MIND-STRUCTURE of a person to a situation; a mindset can be defined as the fixed mental attitude or disposition that determines a person's response, action or behavior to a situation with his own interpretation. It is the structure of one's mind toward circumstances. Phronesis is the action or prudenct wisdom and so it is called the PRACTICAL WISDOM. It is what the person is made of, to do according to situations or circumstances. It is the practical application of the wisdom of God, i.e. the end point of the wisdom of God.

15. WISDOM HAS TYPES

WISDOM OF THIS WORLD *(JAMES 3:14-15)*

This is the wisdom that is operated in the world. It is the system by which the world is structured, directed and guided. This is sensual; i.e. it is according to the natural that is, the senses of the flesh. It is wisdom derived from what seems good to the senses; (sight, smell, taste, hear and touch). It is earthly; that is, it is natural or terrestrial. It obeys the rules of nature, guidelines of nature and the directions of nature. These are the theorems, laws, predictions and postulations of the physical nature. It is also devilish; of the Devil. It has Satan at its peak to blind and deceive the people of the world into darkness *(2Cor 4:4)* this wisdom is foolishness to the wisdom of God *(1Cor 1:20)*; that is, the best (wisest) of the wisdom of this earth is still foolishness to God.

WISDOM OF MEN *(1Cor 2:4-5)*

This is the wisdom that man derived from the wisdom of this world, to make his own wisdom. It is man's conception and perception of the wisdom of the world. The philosophies, reasonings, intellectual thoughts, traditions and rudiments of the world are all the wisdom of man. *(Col 2:8; Beware lest any man spoil you through philosophy and vain deceit, after the tradition of men, after the rudiments of the world, and not after Christ.* This wisdom is also foolishness *(1Cor 1:25, Rom. 1:22)*. It is also sensual i.e. it is judged by the carnal nature (1Cor 2:4).

WISDOM OF GOD *(1Cor 2:7)*

The wisdom of God is the supernatural, true and ultimate wisdom.

This is God's way of doing things. The wisdom of God emanates from the mind of God. It is the way that God thinks and the way that God performs. This wisdom was a mystery, a secret; the hidden wisdom *(1Cor 2:7)* which God had a long time kept to himself and concealed from the world; but now is revealed to the saints *(Col 1:26)* by the spirit of God*(1Cor 2:10)*.

It is first Pure, then peaceable, gentle and easy to be entreated, full of mercy and good fruit, without partiality and without hypocrisy. *(James 3:17)*. Every believer has the access to the wisdom of God to function in him. We have been bestowed with the fullness of God's wisdom as a promise of our salvation through his Son; He has so given unto us without measure (i.e. bountifully). So if any man that lacks this, he should ask of God that gives liberally to ALL men *(James 1:5)* but with a reverence in his heart, for the fear of the lord is the beginning of wisdom. As a living soul in Christ, we will discuss more on the wisdom of God, neglecting other forms of wisdom.

16. WISDOM IS THE FOUNDATION OF ALL THINGS

John 1:3; All things were made by Him; and without Him was anything made that was made.

In explanation of this scripture, all things were made by him. He was with God, not only so as to be acquainted with the divine counsels from eternity, but to be active in the divine operations in the beginning of time. Then was I by him, *Prov. 8:30.* God made the world by a word *(Psa. 33:6)* and Christ was the Word. By him, not as a subordinate instrument, but as a co-ordinate agent, God made the world *(Heb.1:2),* not as the workman cuts by his axe, but as the body sees by the eye. The contrary is denied: Without him was not anything made that was made, from the highest angel to the worm. God the Father did nothing without him in that work. Now, this proves that He is God; for He that built all things is God, *Heb. 3:4.* The God of Israel often proved Himself to be God with this, that He made all things: *Isa. 40:12, Isa. 40:28; Isa. 41:4; and see Jer. 10:11, Jer. 10:12.* This proves the Excellency of the Christian lifestyle, that the author and founder of it is the same that was the author and founder of the world. How excellent must that constitution be which derives its institution from him who is the fountain of all Excellency! When we worship Christ, we worship him to whom the patriarchs gave honor as the Creator of the world, and on whom all creatures depend. This shows how well qualified He was for the work of our redemption and salvation. Help was laid upon one that was mighty indeed; for it was laid upon Him that made all things; and he is appointed the author of our bliss who was the author of our being. No building takes a shape better than the foundation you give to it. In the modern world of today we see lots and lots of great buildings being erected, buildings with great heights and shapes, you will agree with me that none of these buildings are better than their foundation, in other words a building is not better than its foundation. *Isaiah 28:16: therefore thus saith the lord God, Behold, I lay in Zion for a foundation a stone, a tried Stone ,a precious corner stone, a sure foundation: he that believeth shall not make haste. 1 pet 2:6: wherefore also it is contained in the scripture, Behold, I lay in Zion a chief corner stone, elect, precious: and he that believeth on him shall not be confounded. 1 Cor. 3:11:* for other foundation can no man lay than that is laid, which is Jesus Christ. Like I was saying earlier every foundation determines every building, and do not forget that what makes a foundation strong is the nature of the material used. Wisdom is Christ and Christ is the foundation of everything both the seen and the unseen. When you came into Christ you received wisdom as your foundation...but you also build on it using wisdom which is also Christ.

17. WISDOM IS CHRIST

1Cor. 1:30: But of him are ye in Christ Jesus, who of God is made unto us wisdom, and righteousness, and sanctification, and redemption: Wisdom is a person and that person is Christ, therefore to understand the wisdom of God we must understand the person of Christ. The word Christ came from the Greek word Christos which means "the anointed". *1 John 1:20: But ye have an unction from the holy one, and ye know all things.* Looking at that scripture you will see that it spoke of an unction which can also mean the anointing which gives knowledge about all things. How did this anointing come? It comes at the new birth, immediately when you give your life to the person of Jesus you receive this anointing. You must understand that what makes Jesus peculiar was the anointing that was given unto him without measure *(Acts 10:38)* I hope you understand now what Christ means? Now what does wisdom have to do with the Christ? Remember I said earlier that Christ is the wisdom of God, then let me say if you have received Christ then you have received all the wisdom of God, but howbeit in your spirit man. You have all the wisdom of God in your spirit, but your soul needs to learn how to exercise this wisdom, your soul needs to learn how to function in this wisdom, your spirit is fully saved, your soul is being saved, and your body will be saved...this tends to sum up to the fact that the more of Christ you get into your soul the more of the wisdom you can manifest.

18. WISDOM IS LIGHT

John 1:8-10; [8] *He was not that Light, but was sent to bear witness of that Light.* [9] *That was the true Light which gives light to every man coming into the world.* [10] *He was in the world, and the world was made through Him, and the world did not know Him.*

Light is a thing which witnesses for itself through it's illumination and lightening capacity, and carries its own evidence along with it; but to those who shut their eyes against the light it is necessary there should be those that bear witness to it. Christ's light needs not man's testimony, but the world's darkness does. John was like the night watchman that goes round the town, proclaiming the approach of the morning light to those that have closed their eyes, and are not willing themselves to observe it; or like that watchman that was set to tell those who asked him what of the night that the morning comes, and, if you will enquire, enquire ye, *Isa. 21:11, Isa. 21:12.* He was sent of God to tell the world that the long-looked-for Messiah was now come, who should be a light to enlighten the Gentiles and the glory of his people Israel; and to proclaim that dispensation at hand which would bring life and immortality to light. The design of his testimony: That all men through him might believe; not in him, but in Christ, whose way he was sent to prepare. Christ was the true Light not as if John the Baptist were a false light, but, in comparison with Christ, he was a very small light. Christ is the great light that deserves to be called so. Other lights are but figuratively and equivocally called so: Christ is the true light. The fountain of all knowledge and of all comfort must needs be the true light. He is the true light, and we are rays of that light, which are darted downwards, and with which this dark world of ours is enlightened. But how does Christ enlighten every man that comes into the world? By his creating power he enlightens every man with the light of reason; that life which is the light of men is from him; all the discoveries and directions of reason, all the comfort it gives us, and all the beauty it puts upon us, are from Christ. By the publication of his gospel to all nations he does in effect enlighten every man. John the Baptist was a light, but he enlightened only Jerusalem and Judea, and the region round about Jordan, like a candle that enlightens one room; but Christ is the true light, for he is a light to enlighten the Gentiles. His everlasting gospel is to be preached to every nation and language, *Rev. 14:6*. Like the sun which enlightens every man that will open his eyes, and receive its light *(Psa.19:6; its rising is from one end of heaven, and its circuit to the other end; and there is nothing hidden from its heat),* to which the preaching of the gospel is compared. See *Rom.10:18*. Divine revelation is not now to be confined, as it had been, to one people, but to be diffused to all people, *Matt. 5:15*. By the operation of his Spirit and grace he enlightens all those that are enlightened to salvation; and those that are not enlightened by him perish in darkness. The light of the knowledge of the glory of God is said to be in the face of Jesus Christ, and is compared with that light which was at the beginning commanded to shine out of darkness, and which enlightens every man that comes into the world. Whatever light any man has, he is indebted to Christ for it, whether it be natural or supernatural. Wisdom is Christ, Christ is the light of the world. *John 8:12; Then Jesus spoke to them again, saying, "I am the light of the world. He who follows me shall not walk in darkness, but have the light of life."*

19. WISDOM IS LIFE

John 1:4; In Him was life, and the life was the light of men.

Wisdom has life in himself; not only the true one, but the living one. Wisdom is life; he swears by himself when he said, as I live. All living creatures have their life in him; not only all the matter of the creation was made by him, but all the life too that is in the creation is derived from him and supported by him. It was the Word of God that produced the moving creatures that had life, *Gen.1:20; Acts. 17:25.* He is that Word by which man lives more than by bread, *Mat. 4:4.* Reasonable creatures have their light from him; that life which is the light of men comes from him. Life in man is something greater and nobler than it is in other creatures; it is rational, and not merely animal. When man became a living soul, his life was light, his capacities such as distinguished him and dignified him above, the beasts that perish. The spirit of a man is the candle of the Lord, and it was the eternal Word that lighted this candle. The light of reason, as well as the life of sense, is derived from him, and depends upon him. This proves him fit to undertake our salvation; for life and light, spiritual and eternal life and light, are the two great things that fallen man, who lies so much under the power of death and darkness, has need of. From whom may we better expect the light of divine revelation than from him who gave us the light of human reason? And if, when God gave us natural life, that life was in his Son, how readily should we receive the gospel-record that he hath given us eternal life, and that life too is in his Son. *1John5:11- 12;* [11] *and this is the testimony: that God has given us eternal life, and this life is in His Son.* [12] *He who has the Son has life; he who does not have the Son of God does not have life.*

20.WISDOM IS MULTI-FACETED

Ps. 104:24; O Lord, how manifold are your works! In wisdom you have made them all. The earth is full of your possessions.

Eph. 3:10; to the intent that now the manifold wisdom of God might be made known by the church to the principalities and powers in the heavenly places,

This was one thing, among others, which God had in his eye in revealing this mystery, that the good angels, who have a pre-eminence in governing the kingdoms and principalities of the world, and who are endued with great power to execute the will of God on this earth (though their ordinary residence is in heaven) may be informed, from what passes in the church and is done in and by it, of the manifold wisdom of God; that is, of the great variety with which God wisely dispenses things, or of his wisdom manifested in the many ways and methods he takes in ordering his church in the several ages of it, and especially in receiving the Gentiles into it. The holy angels, who look into the mystery of our redemption by Christ, could not but take notice of this branch of that mystery that among the Gentiles is preached the unsearchable riches of Christ. And this is according to the eternal purpose which he purposed in Christ Jesus our Lord. The operation of wisdom is multi-dimensional.

21. GOD OWNS AND GIVES WISDOM

Pro 2:6; For the LORD gives wisdom: out of his mouth cometh knowledge and understanding.

It is always impossible to give what you don't have, the ability of a person to bestow a gift upon a person is in the possession of such gift. God is a being who is full of wisdom because he is wisdom himself. Christ is the fullness of God's wisdom, he owns the very definition of wisdom. *1Ti 1:17; Now unto the King eternal, immortal, invisible, the only wise God, be honor and glory for ever and ever. Amen.* He is the all wise God, having a super intelligence that is more than what the earth and the creations in it can comprehend. His total being is full of just one gene which is wisdom. In beholding his majestic power, the only thing that can accurately define him is wisdom because it is just impossible to understand how a being can dwell in light, establishing the earth by the very word of his and even sustain it by that power. Because he is the fullness of this wisdom, he owns it and none can ever compare to him in possession of these great treasures. He never bought the wisdom from any one, his life and being, expressions in gifts, judgments, etc. are naturally wisdom and it is impossible to live without his wisdom. "God is not the all wise God only, He is the 'only wise' God", he is never in competition with any man. The highest wisdom of man is foolishness unto him because he owns that very wisdom and to possess such, you must seek his wisdom. One very striking characteristic of this God is that, he has purposed in his heart to give of his wisdom. He is not a selfish God and not only does he give, he gives liberally, according to his ever willing mercy and grace. *James 1:5; if any of you lack wisdom, let him ask of God, that giveth to all men liberally, and upbraided not; and it shall be given him.* As a Christian, one of the very great provisions of God's grace at salvation is wisdom, that is, his super intelligence, his ability to create and recreate, build and establish, get good treasure. He that thinks he lacks is always welcome to ask of him, believing in his holy name. Because he understands that it is impossible for man to live a victorious life, doing all of God's will without possessing that intelligence. In living in this world, it is necessary that man has an understanding and deep knowledge of what is uncommon to the human nature. The reason is because, this world was created by the wisdom of God and to understand it, it must be by the wisdom of God. This super intelligence can only be gotten from one man and he gives it as he is asked of from his abundant source which is himself. *Dan 2:21; he changes the times and the seasons: he removes kings, and sets up kings: he gives wisdom unto the wise, and knowledge to them that have understanding:*

22. WISDOM SPEAKS

The wisdom of God is not just a thing, substance, dimension or concept developed to envelope our brain into believing something mystical. The wisdom of God is the very person of God, he is the very eternal life sent to us to proclaim liberty to creation and lifting away bondage from the land. The strongest characteristics of wisdom is that he is a person.

1Cor. 1:24; But unto them which are called, both Jews and Greeks, Christ the power of God, and the wisdom of God. Understanding that the wisdom of God is the person of Christ, then it is necessary that we conclude that the wisdom of God speaks, giving out doses of information from his unfathomable super intelligence and abilities. One of the gravest mistakes of man is to believe that wisdom is just an intelligence, this diminishes the value, and personality of wisdom. One thing we must understand is that all actions that we see (which we call wisdom) are just the expressions or the speaking of wisdom. Those expressions proceed out of a particular source which is wisdom. This unfathomable reality is a personality who doles out his riches in kind, gestures proceeding by his love and mercy towards creation. This individual (wisdom) speaks to our heart when we are in need.

23. WISDOM MADE THE HEAVENS

Psa. 33:6; by the word of the LORD were the heavens made; and all the host of them by the breath of his mouth. Imagine a cosmopolitan environment where everything is so right, living going accordingly as it was proposed. The populace understanding what to do and no confusion setting in. Ever wondered how a firmament can stay in the clouds and not fall, visible to the human eyes but far from our touch. Near to us in sight but extreme to us in handling. Travelling into spaces by our different crafts, wanting to touch the very firmament that is called the heaven but unable to reach that substance. How is it possible that a substance is seen by the physical eyes but can only be accessed by the spiritual minds. Some believe we have Seven heavens, some believe we have only three. But the conglomeration of spaces beats the human calculations of mathematical distance or bearings. Our cursors tries to find out the degree to which we can travel, rockets have been launched, running at its fastest speed, so as just to touch this world that is of little knowledge to us. How can a world be that houses spirits, conglomerations of them, even more than the earth has ever recorded, having the stars and the moon as friends but never revealing its very nature and source to the human nature.

The specimens of what the heavens is can be re-examined over and over again but will never yield scientific results. The reason is because, in creation and establishment of this very world is hidden a particular substance of the majesty, "wisdom".

Jer. 10:12; He hath made the earth by his power, he hath established the world by his wisdom, and hath stretched out the heavens by his discretion. The very substance that created this wonder is the wisdom of God, the super intelligence of God. He made heavens and hid them in a heaven. He made spirits and put them in a world of their own far from the human eyes. He established a world and made it accessible to all by a particular spiritual channel, spaces that beat the human imagination, lands that can never be calculated by any genius mathematician, even its existence and beginning is hidden facts, the arrangements of powers, principalities, thrones, names, etc. beats the very important and royal arrangement of the greatest earth kingdom that ever existed or will ever exist. This very heaven was crafted and established by the wisdom of God, even they are sustained by that same wisdom.

Neh. 9:6; Thou, even thou, art LORD alone; thou hast made heaven, the heaven of heavens, with all their host, the earth, and all things that are therein, the seas, and all that is therein, and thou preserves them all; and the host of heaven worships thee. Ps. 136:5; to him that by wisdom made the heavens: for his mercy endures forever.

24. WISDOM CAN BE KNOWN

1Cor. 2:7; but we speak the wisdom of God in a mystery, even the hidden wisdom, which God ordained before the world unto our glory: The ever super intelligence of God is hid in a mystical world. It's a mystery that is not accessible to all or just any man. The stature and technicality of wisdom is great and there is need for special qualifications to know and understand this wisdom. Truth be told, it is possible to know wisdom but there are qualifications; Know the source of wisdom;

Jude 1:25; to the only wise God our Savior, be glory and majesty, dominion and power, both now and ever. Amen. From previous learning, we understand that the very source of wisdom is God himself. The man that has his life and expressions full of wisdom. He cannot be compared to any and he is the very source of that wisdom. The first step to knowing wisdom is knowing He that gives wisdom. "GOD". He can be known by believing and accepting his son whom he sent, *John 3:16; For God so loved the world that he gave his only begotten Son, that whosoever believeth in him should not perish, but have everlasting life.* Stay by the man of wisdom; one very striking thing about wisdom is that it can only be communicated among the mature, that is, for you to have full expressions of this wisdom in understanding and expression, you must have become fully grown. This kind of stature can only be attained by staying with the man of wisdom by constantly communicating with him both from his word and prayer. At this place of fellowshipping, you can always ask of him that gives wisdom liberally to every man that ask of him.

Listen to the Holy Ghost;

1Cor. 2:7; But we speak the wisdom of God in a mystery, even the hidden wisdom, which God ordained before the world unto our glory:

1Cor. 2:8; which none of the princes of this world knew: for had they known it, they would not have crucified the Lord of glory.

1Cor. 2:9; But as it is written, Eye hath not seen, nor ear heard, neither have entered into the heart of man, the things which God hath prepared for them that love him.

1Co 2:10; But God hath revealed them unto us by his Spirit: for the Spirit searches all things, yea, and the deep things of God.

This wisdom that is hid in a mystery has been given to us as a privilege in the Holy Ghost. When we listen to his spirit, we are given access into this wisdom and we just know and understand the unfathomable intelligence of him who established the heavens and the earth. Let's understand that God not only wants us to know and understand this wisdom but we should be able to live by this wisdom and even communicate it when needs arises.

1Cor. 2:6; howbeit we speak wisdom among them that are perfect: yet not the wisdom of this world, nor of the princes of this world, that come to nought:

25. WISDOM BRINGS GLORY

God giving anything to humans is always for a particular purpose, the mind-set of God in giving out gifts is always for the purpose for profiting. Fruit(s) been brought out so as to show the very nature and splendor of such gift.

Also in the gift of wisdom to mankind by God, it is always expedient to understand the reason which is to bear the nature of the man of wisdom himself unto his glory.

1Cor. 2:7; but we speak the wisdom of God in a mystery, even the hidden wisdom, which God ordained before the world unto our glory: Let us understand that wisdom does not come alone, it always comes with a particular glory or for a particular glory. The very essence of the expressions of wisdom is to ascribe the glory to himself and not any other;

Rom 16:27; To God "only wise", be "glory" through Jesus Christ forever. Amen

Jude 1:25; to the "only wise" God our Savior, be "glory" and majesty, dominion and power, both now and ever. Amen.

1Tim 1:17; Now unto the King eternal, immortal, invisible, the "only wise" God, be honor and "glory" for ever and ever. Amen. Glory is the splendor that exudes from a particular expression, the honor that is ascribed to a thing due to its ability to surpass the knowledge of an individual or a thing. Because the wisdom of God is the only wise thing that exists, none other can beat him and his expressions cannot be grasped by human understandings in all their learnings. Therefore any place that wisdom is demonstrated, men will always bow and ascribe honor and worship to the manifestation. Joseph in the scriptures is an example of such, throughout the land of the greatest empire, no wise man could interpret the dream of the king but in his misery, the wisdom of God was demonstrated in Joseph and the result was his promotion to Prime minister and a recognition by the land of Egypt, the power of the great God who dwells and manifests in wisdom. Any individual that can manifest wisdom will surely be honored. Because a man of wisdom is an elder, able to sight problems give solutions to all matters, conquering the deceptive nature of man by his every word and ideas. A man whose word just doesn't drop on the ground because they are important, logical to the processing mind and a mystery to the ordinary minds (needing more digging to understand). The end and preordination of every man by God is a life of virtue, honor and glory. A life that is embedded in his eternal life which is expressed in wisdom, all men need to do is to tap into this source, understand the life, live that kind of life, and walk his way to the preordained land of glory.

FORTHCOMING BOOKS BY ALPHONSO CRAWFORD:

LIFE'S WAY UNTIL: POEMS ON FAITH/HOPE/SALVATION

TWO HEARTS: LOVE POEMS/LOVE LETTERS

CROSSROADS: POEMS ON RACE/POLITICS/LIFE

100 WAYS FOR PEOPLE TO GET HEALED

100 SYMBOLS OF HEALTH AND HEALING

ADVANCED HEALING MANUAL

THE THREE GREATEST CHALLENGES OF LIFE

DOMINATE: 25 DOMINION PRINCIPLES

WHY GOD MADE BLACK PEOPLE BLACK: 25 REASONS

LEADERSHIP IN AN AGE OF CRISIS: 25 OBSERVATIONS

LEADERSHIP: 25 FACTS ABOUT LEADERS

LEADERSHIP: 25 PITFALLS/POWERTOOLS

LEADERSHIP: 25 TOUGH QUESTIONS/TOUGH ANSWERS

WISDOM PERSPECTIVES: 25 INSIGHTS

WISDOM: 25 FACTS ABOUT WISDOM

GOD'S WILL: 25 WAYS TO KNOW GOD'S WILL FOR YOUR LIFE

POWER: 25 FACTS ABOUT POWER

WISDOM ILLUSTRATED

POWERS THAT WOMEN POSSESS

ADVANCED INTERPERSONAL COMMUNICATION: 25 WAYS TO EXPRESS YOURSELF

DREAMS: 25 FEATURES OF DREAMS

THE POWER OF BIG THINKING: 25 LAWS

SPIRITUOTHERAPY: 25 PRINCIPLES

MEN: 25 FACTS ABOUT MEN

HEART: 25 FACTS ABOUT THE HEART

PERSONALITY PROFILES: A BIBLICAL PERSPECTIVE

HEALTH AND HEALING DEVOTIONAL BOOK

HEALTH AND HEALING AFFIRMATIONBOOK

BLOOD: 25 FACTS ABOUT THE BLOOD

HEALTH AND HEALING QUIZ BOOK

HEALTH AND HEALING WORKBOOK: 25 ACTIVITIES

FORTHCOMING BOOKS BY ELEANOR CRAWFORD

WOMEN IN MINISTRY: 25 WAYS TO IMPACT THE WORLD

WOMEN: 25 FACTS ABOUT WOMEN

WOMEN: 25 WOMEN THAT CHANGED HISTORY

WOMEN'S RESOURCES: 25 ASSETS

WOMEN OF DESTINY: 25 CHALLENGES

WOMEN OF WISDOM: 25 INSIGHTS

WOMEN'S MANUAL: 25 LIFE LESSONS

WOMEN'S WORKBOOK: 25 ACTIVITIES

WOMEN'S DEVOTIONAL BOOK

WOMEN'S AFFIRMATION BOOK

WOMENS' SERMONS: 25 SERMONS

WOMEN AND MEN: 25 CONTRASTS

FORTHCOMING BOOKS BY BYRON CRAWFORD

SELL YOUR WAY TO SUCCESS: 25 WAYS TO SUCCEED IN LIFE

LAWS OF SUCCESS: 25 PRINCIPLES

SUCCESS SECRETS: 25 SECRETS

SYNONYMS FOR SUCCESS: 25 CORRELATIONS

SUCCESS MANUAL: 25 LIFE LESSONS

SUCCESS WORKBOOK: 25 POWERFUL ACTIVITIES

SUCCESSFUL STRATEGIC PLANNING: 25 TACTICS

SUCCESS SERMONS: 25 SUCCESS SERMONS

SUCCESS QUIZ BOOK

SUCCESS DEVOTIONAL BOOK

SUCCESS AFFIRMATION BOOK

SIGN UP AND BE NOTIFIED FOR SEMINARS/ WORKSHOPS/CONFERENCES

NAME_____

ADDRESS_____

CITY_____

STATE_____ZIP CODE_____

PHONE NO._____

EMAIL ADDRESS_____

SEND TO:

NEW LIFE EDUCATIONAL SERVICES
P.O. BOX 96
OAK LAWN, ILLINOIS 60454

SEMINARS/WORKSHOPS/CONFERENCES

- ANNUAL WOMENS' CONFERENCE

- HEALTH AND HEALING

- DREAMS AND VISIONS

- PERSONAL POWER

- GIFTS AND TALENTS

- RELATIONSHIPS

- PROBLEM SOLVING

- HOW TO START A BUSINESS

- FIVEFOLD MINISTRY

- INTERPRETING CURRENT TRENDS

- ADVANCED INTERPERSONAL COMMUNICATION

- ADVANCED STRATEGIC PLANNING

- MANAGING SELF

- MANAGING CONFLICT

- MANAGING STRESS

- LAWS OF POWER

- ANNUAL MENS' CONFERENCE

- NEGOTIATION SKILLS

- ANNUAL MENS' CONFERENCE

- BIG THINKING POWER

- STRATEGIES FOR SUCCESS

- HOW TO SELL YOURSELF

- THE DYNAMICS OF PURPOSE

- GLOBAL STEWARDSHIP

- HOW TO COUNSEL

- SELF MOTIVATION

- PEOPLE MOTIVATION

- SPIRITUAL EXERCISES

- LIFE SKILLS

- TEAM BUILDING

- APOSTOLIC/PROPHETIC CONFERENCE

- HOW TO START A CHRISTIAN SCHOOL

- HOW TO HOME SCHOOL

- SELF DECEPTION: HOW WE LIE TO OURSELVES EVERYDAY

- VISION

- TIME MANAGEMENT

- SETTING GOALS

- CHANGE AGENTS

- HOW TO BECOME A CONSULTANT

- WEALTH IN YOU

- FEEDBACK

- NEEDS OF WOMEN AND MEN

ABOUT THE AUTHOR

Dr. Crawford is an Apostle of health and healing. Dr. Crawford is the president of New Life Educational Services. He pastors Cathedral Of Prayer with his wife. Dr. Crawford received his background in biblical studies from Moody Bible Institute. He has a B.A. from DePaul University, the Master Of Divinity from McCormick Theological Seminary, the Doctor Of Ministry from Chicago Theological Seminary respectively at the University Of Chicago.

CONCLUSION

The person of wisdom is the person of Christ and He is a Spirit in believers. *Jesus Christ is the same yesterday, today, and forever. (Heb. 13:8).* The Wisdom of God has been the same through all ages and He will remain the same forever but his ways and manners are dynamic in the realm of God.

www.ingramcontent.com/pod-product-compliance
Lightning Source LLC
Chambersburg PA
CBHW060429050426
42449CB00009B/2210